Original title:
Happiness in the Christmas Stars

Author: Eleanor Prescott
ISBN HARDBACK: 978-9916-90-984-3
ISBN PAPERBACK: 978-9916-90-985-0

Christmas Dreams Under a Canopy of Wonder

In the attic, old Santa stares,
With a list of names and too many flares.
He's checking it twice, but oh the plight,
He forgot the cookies and milk last night!

Rudolph's nose is quite the show,
But that nose can trip you; don't say you know!
He dances around, but takes a fall,
'Not my fault!' he honks, 'I heard the call!'

The tree is up, a sparkling sight,
But the cat thinks it's a new kind of height.
She climbs and she tumbles, oh what a fright,
Now the ornaments are a cat's delight!

Grandma's wreath is a bit askew,
The cat brought it down; who knew?
Now it's a crown on her furry head,
'Tis the season for laughs instead!

So hang up the stockings, watch them sway,
For Christmas dreams are on display.
With laughter and joy wrapped up tight,
We'll celebrate this magical night!

Starlit Whispers of Delight

Under the stars, my cat took flight,
With dreams of catching a comet tonight.
But the comet just laughed, said, 'Not my style,'
As my cat came down, looking sheepish and vile.

The moon winked bright, 'What a silly sight!'
A dance of the planets, all to the right.
But the best part was when Jupiter sneezed,
And the stars giggled softly, all quite amused.

The Glow of Festive Dreams

In the fridge, a pie did cheerfully sing,
While the turkey wore a festive gold ring.
Mittens for paws, our dog joins the feast,
Dreaming of dancing with a friend, the big beast.

The lights twinkle bright, like stars on the ground,
As we jive on the table, what fun we'd found!
With fruitcake that bounced like a beach ball absurd,
Everyone chortles at dessert's odd word.

Shimmering Echoes of Hope

A goldfish in glasses, quite wise and spry,
Told me to never stop reaching the sky.
With bubbles of joy and winks so profound,
He promised me ceaseless good fortune abound.

The snail next door, slow but full of dreams,
Raced past my house, or so it seems.
He laughed as he traveled, quite jaunty and grand,
Said, 'Life's much more fun when you're never quite
planned.'

Celestial Laughter Above

The sun cracked a joke right before it set,
Said, 'I'm the best star, don't you forget!'
While the clouds rolled by, grinning ear to ear,
They traded some puns that were quite insincere.

Stars twinkled back, in a cosmic conga,
Reflecting on jokes that just kept getting longer.
In the night sky, where humor takes flight,
Each laugh was a rocket, delighting the night.

Celebrating Moments of Radiance

Oh, look at me, in my fine new hat,
I tripped on a cat, now I'm stuck in a mat.
With cake on my face and joy in my heart,
This party's a blast, I'll now play the part.

Inflatable unicorns float by with glee,
They tried to join in a dance, but much to my spree,
They popped in their joy, what a sight to behold,
Now it's cake and confetti, a true moment gold!

Dancing Among the Heavenly Lanterns.

We twirl with lanterns, just floating along,
But check out that one – oh no, it's too strong!
It's pulling us up, we're flying away,
Look down, we've left snacks, oh what a bad day!

The moon's laughing hard, he's cracked up like me,
Forgetting our shoes, we land in a tree.
With giggles and wiggles, we laugh till we drop,
Dancing with lanterns, we'll never stop!

Whispers of Joy Beneath Winter Skies

In winter's embrace, we build up a snow,
A snowman so big, he steals all the show.
But wait, what's that? He's started to dance!
A jig in the snow, oh, we're taking a chance!

The whispers of joy float up through the cold,
With mittens and laughter, a joy to behold.
As snowflakes come down, wrapping all in white,
We'll twirl and we'll spin 'til the fall of the night.

A Dance of Light in the Frosted Night

The stars have come out, it's quite the grand sight,
We're dancing with shadows, all filled with delight.
But tripped on a star, oh what a big blunder,
We whirled through the sky, like we were in thunder!

With lights all around, we giggle and glide,
Each twinkling wish, we cannot quite hide.
In frosted delight, with giggles that chime,
We dance on through the night, losing all sense of time!

Mirthful Moments in Crisp Air

The sun is bright, the air is cool,
We frolic like we're back in school.
A snowball fight, oh what a thrill,
With laughter echoing up the hill.

Hot cocoa waits in mugs so wide,
With marshmallows that bob and glide.
We watch the snowflakes swirl and twirl,
As winter's charms begin to unfurl.

Let's build a snowman, tall and round,
With carrots, buttons, laughter around.
But in his face, a cat we see,
He swiped our hat, oh woe is me!

So here's to joy in frosty air,
To playful moments, love and care.
We'll dance and sing, our spirits bright,
In winter's arms, from morn till night.

A Tinsel Glow in the Midnight Hour

The clock strikes twelve, the lights all shine,
We gather close with mugs of wine.
The tree adorned in tinsel glow,
With sparkles twinkling in the snow.

A cat named Mittens steals the show,
He knocks the bulbs, oh look at him go!
With ornaments rolling on the floor,
We laugh so hard, who could ask for more?

A dance-off starts with funny moves,
As Auntie twirls, her hippos groove.
Uncle Joe falls flat, what a scene,
We roll in laughter, oh it's serene!

So raise your glass, let's toast tonight,
To mirth and madness, what a delight!
For in this glow, we find our cheer,
With love and laughter, year after year.

Kindred Souls Beneath the Glittering Canopy

Beneath the stars, our secrets shared,
With dreams and giggles, nothing bared.
We skip the serious, dive in fun,
As shooting stars in silence run.

Each story told, a belly ache,
From laughing hard, oh what a rake!
Friendship's warmth, a cozy fire,
With marshmallow toasting—our hearts admire.

A snow-white squirrel joins our chat,
He takes our snacks, the little brat!
We shoo him off, but he returns,
For tasty treats, the little burns.

So here's to nights of joy and play,
With kindred souls, come what may.
Beneath the stars, our spirits soar,
In nature's arms, we find our core.

A Winter's Tale of Warm Embrace

The wind is howling, the snowflakes dance,
We cozy up in our knit romance.
With blankets piled high, a movie spree,
The cat curls up, oh can't you see?

A popcorn fight breaks out with glee,
As half the bowl ends up on me!
We flick the remotes, change the scene,
The Christmas story—oh so serene.

With hot pies baking, scents divine,
We sneak a slice, just one more time!
And then we giggle, both a mess,
From sticky fingers, what a stress!

So here's to winter, warm and bright,
With laughter echoing through the night.
In every hug, a tale retraced,
In winter's arms, we're interlaced.

Sledding Through Waves of Delighted Light

Down the hill, we slide with glee,
Spinning like tops, so wild and free.
In our sleds, we zoom and dart,
Falling off gives winter its art!

Snowflakes dance upon our heads,
Landing softly, like fluffy beds.
We tumble, we roll, we laugh so hard,
Who knew winter would be this wild card!

Winter's Canvas: A Tapestry of Bliss

The ground is white, like frosting spread,
Snowmen sprout, with carrots for heads.
A snowball fight breaks out with a cheer,
We launch our icy missiles, oh dear!

Hot cocoa waits, it's calling our name,
With marshmallows floating, it's quite the game.
Winter's here, let's shout hurray,
Before we freeze our toes away!

Chasing the Glimmer of Enchanted Nights

Stars twinkle like diamonds in the sky,
We chase fireflies, oh my, oh my!
The night is young, the moon's a-bloom,
We dance in the dark, try not to zoom!

Every shadow plays peek-a-boo,
With giggles and whispers, just us two.
In the chill, we find our delight,
Chasing the glimmer of the enchanted night.

Radiant Smiles Beneath the North Star

Up in the sky, the North Star shines,
While we share laughter over sipping wines.
Our cheeks are rosy, our hearts are bright,
Making memories under twinkling light.

We dance in circles, we sing our song,
In this winter wonder, we all belong.
Radiant smiles, like snowflakes, we bear,
Living for moments we love to share!

Twinkling Joys of the Winter Sky

Snowflakes dance, oh what a sight,
They land on noses, a comical bite.
Snowmen wobble, hats askew,
With carrots that say, "I see you!"

Kids dart out, ready to play,
Sleds in tow, hip-hip-hooray!
While parents sip cocoa, warm and nice,
Secretly wishing for summer's spice.

Fingers get cold, but laughter is hot,
Near a snow fort, a snowy spot.
Snowball fights bring giggles and squeals,
In this winter wonderland that twirls on wheels!

Stars above in a blanket of night,
Twinkling like laughter, pure delight.
Winter's joy is a frosty cheer,
Let's keep it rolling, all through the year!

A Serenade of Light and Cheer

In the night, the lights do glow,
Twinkling softly, putting on a show.
Dance like fairies, bright and bold,
Singing stories of joy untold.

Tinsel drapes, hanging with flair,
Cats get tangled without a care.
Ornaments jingle, a merry tune,
Under the watch of a chocolate moon.

Whiskers twitch from behind the tree,
Is that a gift just for me?
The puppy steals a roll of wrap,
Unwrapping chaos in a happy nap.

Hot cocoa flows like a river wide,
Marshmallows bob, let's take a ride!
A serenade of light, we cheer,
Laughter and love, the best of the year!

Beneath the Frosted Wishes

Beneath the stars, the world is still,
Frosty wishes chase up the hill.
A snowflake whispered, 'make a wish,'
As penguins bobbed, feeling delish.

Sleds go crashing, oh what a thrill,
Parents sigh while kids climb the hill.
Snowball launches, a perfect arc,
Landing on dad's hat with a spark!

Candy canes dance on the dining table,
With gingerbread men, oh so stable.
Cookies vanish, a sweet retreat,
A frosted wonder, a tasty feat!

So gather 'round, the joy we'll share,
Beneath the frost, love's floating air.
With laughter echoing all around,
In winter's arms, happiness is found!

Threads of Gold in the Night

As the sun sets, colors ignite,
Threads of gold weave through the night.
Stars start to sprinkle, a cosmic quilt,
Dreams take flight, as laughter's built.

Dancing snowflakes, each a delight,
While carolers sing, hearts feel light.
Chubby cheeks, rosy and bright,
Chasing the wonders, oh what a sight!

Mittens mismatched, but who cares?
Jumping in snow, how it flares!
With cheeks aglow from a winter kiss,
This frosty world offers such bliss!

So gather your friends, let's take in the scene,
In the glow of the night, we'll laugh and glean.
Threads of gold remind us, take flight,
Together in joy, we shine so bright!

Unwrapping Celestial Blessings

On Christmas Day, I lost my socks,
They vanished like a sly old fox.
Wrapped gifts piled high, all looking great,
But where's my warmth? Oh, this is fate!

A present box with a giant bow,
Something wriggly inside, oh no!
Is it a pet or a booby trap?
I'll find out soon with a funny rap.

The cookies baked, but they came out raw,
A crunchy surprise that made folks guffaw.
Each bite a gamble, a taste of thrill,
Christmas dinner sure is a skill!

So here's to blessings, wrapped tight in cheer,
And goofy moments that bring us near.
With laughter and love, let's toast and sing,
Unwrapping joy, such a silly thing!

Dancing Shadows of Christmas Light

In the night, the shadows prance,
Behind the tree, they take a chance.
Twinkling lights spark a silly jig,
Everyone laughs, it's quite the gig!

The cat leaps high, a festive sight,
Chasing baubles, oh what a fright!
Grandma's sweater sparkles so bright,
Looks like she dressed in Christmas light!

The cookies gone before I could eat,
Santa's magic, can't be beat!
He left a note — 'More milk next year!'
I'll make sure to leave him a whole beer.

So dance we will, with shadows in tow,
Under the mistletoe, all aglow.
With laughter and joy, we'll always ignite,
These dancing shadows bring such delight!

Gleaming Wishes upon the Wind

A wish upon a breeze so sly,
I tossed a coin, it soared on high.
But instead of luck, a pigeon came,
And settled down, I felt quite lame!

Wishes sparkle like tinsel bright,
But how they vanish, out of sight!
I wished for toys, instead got socks,
Oh fa-la-la, my fortune rocks!

In the air, a wish does fly,
But often lands on some poor guy.
Caught in a tree, it makes me grin,
Wishes are fun, but where've they been?

So here's to dreams that tumble and sway,
I'll keep on wishing day by day.
With every chuckle, let's take a spin,
Gleaming wishes caught in the wind!

Love Letters in the Milky Way

In a galaxy far, far away,
Love letters float and dance, they sway.
The aliens giggle as they read,
My Valentine's card—a cosmic deed!

Stars twinkle tales of love's sweet song,
While Martians debate if I'm right or wrong.
With hearts made of stardust, they take my word,
"Romance on Earth? We've totally heard!"

Back on Earth, I sent a kiss,
To my crush, oh what a bliss!
The message zapped through space so fast,
Hoping they'd feel this love at last.

So let's write letters, both near and far,
Send them on rockets, a shooting star.
In the Milky Way, our love will sway,
With laughter and joy, love leads the way!

Radiant Memories on Frosty Mornings

Hot cocoa spills from my mug,
While snowflakes dance like a bug.
Sipping warmth, my cheeks turn red,
Did I remember to eat breakfast instead?

Frosty breath escapes with a puff,
Winter mornings just get tough.
Woolly socks upon my toes,
How do I lose one? Nobody knows!

The dog prances with glee outside,
Wearing his coat, he takes pride.
I trip on snow, fall with style,
Then laugh at my tumble, all the while.

Yet despite the chill, joy swells in me,
These radiant memories, pure glee.
Snowy mornings, a cozy embrace,
With laughter and warmth, my favorite place.

The Joy of Giving Wrapped in Shimmering Light

Packages piled, what a sight,
Bows that shine and glitter bright.
But what's this? A gift for me?
Did I just snag my own spree?

Ribbons tangled, oh what a mess,
Unwrapping reveals, my old dress!
Thoughtful? Sure, but wait, oh dear,
I'm the one who's giving the cheer?

Laughter bubbles as I sigh,
Wrapped in paper, my tears run dry.
A gift of socks? Oh what delight!
Whose idea was this? Mine, alright!

Yet still I smile with all my might,
For joy of giving feels just right.
In shimmering light, we'll all unite,
Giving laughter, wrapped up tight.

Celestial Celebrations Above Festive Fires

Stars twinkle like lights on a tree,
While marshmallows roast, oh glee!
Grandma's stories of ghosts long gone,
While dad tries to turn them into a song.

Fires crackle, sparks jump high,
Someone's hat just flew to the sky!
With laughter echoing through the night,
What's better than this festive sight?

Singing off-key, we jump and dance,
A holiday spirit, we take our chance.
With eggnog spills and too much cheer,
We'll celebrate the whole year!

So let the celestial light shine bright,
As festivities sparkle with sheer delight.
Amidst warm fires, all feel the desire,
To laugh and love—our hearts inspired.

Snowflakes and Starlight in Perfect Harmony

Snowflakes swirl in the moon's soft glow,
With cheeks and noses all aglow.
Starlight twinkles, a perfect scene,
As little elves take on the green.

My snowman wears a hat too high,
As birds fly past with an awkward sigh.
Falling over, I try to stand,
And suddenly I'm buried in snow, oh grand!

Snowball fights erupt with a squeal,
Laughing at hits that seem surreal.
In perfect harmony, friends collide,
While hot chocolate waits as our guide.

So here's to winter with its snowy charms,
Zipping down hills, it always disarms.
With starlight and snowflakes, smiles abound,
In joyful moments, true love is found.

Radiance in December's Embrace

In December's chill, we deck the halls,
With tinsel, lights, and Santa calls.
Elves are busy, making toys,
While reindeer practice, oh what joys!

Hot cocoa spills in festive cheer,
As we toast to friends both far and near.
Snowflakes dance, but they fall slow,
Watch out! A snowball's coming, whoa!

Grandma's fruitcake just made its way,
I think it could be used for clay.
The cat's on the tree, it makes no sense,
We laugh so hard, our breath's immense!

So here's to warmth in winter's grasp,
With chuckles shared, in laughter we clasp.
Radiance beams from each smiling face,
In December's embrace, there's always grace.

Harmony of Snow and Stardust

Snowflakes twirl in moonlight's glow,
Like sparkly dancers in a show.
Stars wink down, they seem to know,
That winter's a quirky little flow.

A snowman's hat is askew on his head,
With carrot nose that's better off dead.
Children giggle, their cheeks all red,
With each funny face, old worries shred.

In the silence, snow whispers sweet,
As stardust falls, we stomp our feet.
Hot chocolate's served, it can't be beat,
Sipping joy until we're obsolete.

So let's embrace this wintry plight,
With laughter echoing into the night.
Harmony sings, both snow and light,
As we frolic until dawn's first sight.

The Gift of Midnight Magic

At midnight, magic starts to play,
With twinkling lights in a grand ballet.
The moon is grinning, it's here to say,
That dreams come true in a wacky way.

Elves in pajamas dance on the roof,
While the cat kicks snowballs—what a goof!
Gifts misnamed with cheeky sleuth,
Surprise! A sweater for a moose, who'd a thought? Proof!

Giggles erupt from a wide-eyed crowd,
When Santa drops in, looking quite proud.
He trips on the rug, oh what a sound!
But laughter unites, the best gift found.

Midnight magic, so bright and bold,
With stories of joy forever told.
In a world of whimsy, none do grow old,
Together we shine, like treasures of gold.

Echoes of Laughter in the Cosmos

In the cosmos, stars are haywire,
With giggles twinkling, they never tire.
Planets joke, like pals in a choir,
As comets zoom, sparks of laughter inspire.

Alien creatures share silly lore,
Trading their hairstyles, oh what a score!
Space floats gently, inviting more,
In this nebula of chuckles galore.

Asteroid belts are racetracks now,
With spaceships zooming, take a bow.
Black holes gulp, oh don't ask how,
The echoes of laughter make time go wow!

So let's raise a toast to the starry night,
With humor that shines, a cosmic delight.
Through space and time, joy takes flight,
In the universe, we share our light.

Dazzling Revelations in the Midwinter's Night

In winter's chill, my nose does freeze,
I swear my breath just froze the breeze.
A snowman winked, he made a joke,
Said, "You're too warm! Get out, you bloke!"

The stars above, they seem to giggle,
As I tumble down and make a wiggle.
A snowball fight turned into pies,
I made a mess with snow in my eyes!

The cocoa's hot, but so's my hat,
A squirrel stole a biscuit, oh, how 'bout that!
I swear he smiled, ran up a tree,
While I just stood, yelling, "Give it back to me!"

Midwinter's night, with laughter loud,
I dance with snowflakes, feeling proud.
If the moon decides to join our spree,
We'll throw a party, just you wait and see!

Enchanted Dreams Under a Canopy of Stars

Under stars, I drift to sleep,
A cow jumped over, no lie, not cheap!
I woke to see a unicorn fly,
Riding a rainbow, oh my, oh my!

The moon played chess with a sleepy cat,
A knight in armor, and a talking brat.
Whispers of dreams scatter like leaves,
As I grab a snack, oh, how it weaves!

Elves in pajamas, sipping their tea,
Said I can't join, 'cause I'm not as free.
So I danced with the shadows, threw a shoe,
And landed right smack where dreams come true!

So if you gaze at the stars tonight,
And you hear laughter that feels just right,
It's just me partying with my crew,
Making wishes, silly dreams, and woo!

Frosty Whispers of Joy in Distant Heights

Frosty mornings and a sneaky grin,
Is that a snowman? Oh wait, it's a twin!
They're plotting a dance with icy glee,
I swear they just winked at me!

Snowflakes whisper, secrets unfurl,
"Why did the igloo get kicked by a girl?"
I chuckle softly, then I reply,
"Because it was too cool to say goodbye!"

Frosty heights with laughter so clear,
Tiptoeing up like I haven't a fear.
A penguin slid down, wearing a hat,
Shouting, "Watch out! This is where it's at!"

In distant heights, where joy takes flight,
We ice-skate giggles, soaring in delight.
So if you hear frosty whispers tonight,
Join the fun, it's a silly sight!

Joyous Secrets Beneath the Glittering Canopy

Beneath the trees, I heard a clatter,
A raccoon danced like he was a platter.
With tinsel tied, he spun around,
While the squirrels cheered him on, profound!

Joyous secrets, giggles galore,
A snowball brigade at the forest door.
Who threw that? I claimed no blame,
As a squirrel yelled, "You're the one to blame!"

The stars above began to hum,
As a bear joined in, looking quite glum.
"Why are you all so keen to play?
Don't you know it's nap time, hey?"

Glittering canopy shining bright,
The woodland sings with sheer delight.
So join the party beneath the moon,
Where laughter spills in a joyous tune!

Glimmers of Bliss Adorning the Frozen Landscape

In winter's chill, I sip hot tea,
I'm dressed like a marshmallow, can't you see?
Snowflakes dance, like tiny sprites,
My nose is red, but my heart's alight.

My snowman's got a carrot nose,
But he's drooping now, I suppose.
With every gust, his hat takes flight,
I chase it down, slipping—what a sight!

Birds are chirping, they seem so bold,
While I'm bundled, feeling old.
They sing and flit without a care,
I wonder if they think I'm rare!

The ice rink's full, kids spin and glide,
I attempt to skate, but simply slide.
I've become a human snowball, it's true,
But laughter fills the air, and joy will ensue.

Fond Remembrance on Starlit Paths

Starlit paths remind me so,
Of silly dances long ago.
I twirled and stumbled, what a sight!
My shadow laughed and took to flight.

Snowmen built with friends galore,
One year, we lost a hat, oh poor!
But what a thrill, we laughed so hard,
Our memories, forever starred.

Chasing snowflakes, little joys,
Each flake a little world, my boys.
They stick their tongues out in wild glee,
I just hope one doesn't get stuck on me!

The stars above twinkle with glee,
As we recount our history.
Sledding down hills, screeching loud,
What happy moments made us proud!

A Tapestry of Joy in the Winter Sky

Patchwork sky of blue and gray,
Snowflakes fall, come out to play.
A squirrel slips, oh what a show,
He's taken out by a veil of snow!

I built a fort, it's time to wage,
A snowball fight, let's hit the stage!
We dodge and weave with shouts of cheer,
The winner gets hot cocoa, oh dear!

Children laughing, voices bright,
Winter's chill can't dampen this light.
With frosty breath, we share our dreams,
While racing down those icy streams.

As twilight falls, we gather 'round,
Sharing stories, joy abound.
In cozy blankets, friends unite,
Our hearts aglow on this winter night.

Songs of Cheer Beneath Celestial Beacons

Under the stars, we gather close,
With mugs of cocoa, we're not morose.
Laughter rings, a joyful song,
Where friendship blooms, we all belong.

The snowflakes twirl; we do a jig,
I trip and fall, but oh so big!
My belly laughs as I land with a thud,
Covered in snow—a soft, white bud.

The moon peeks out, a silver grin,
As nature sighs, we take it in.
With every flake that paints the ground,
We weave our tales, with love, profound.

Celestial beacons light our way,
As we sing together, come what may.
With hearts as warm as fireside glow,
We cherish moments that gently flow.

Glittering Lullabies from Above

The stars twinkle bright like a dazzling show,
With a wink and a nudge, they steal the scene,
Napping on clouds, oh what a cozy row,
Dreams wrapped in sparkles, a magical bean.

The moon hums a tune, a lullaby neat,
As comets dance by, all in a whirl,
Singing with owls, tapping their feet,
A giggle erupts, it's a whimsical twirl.

Bears in pajamas with slippers of fluff,
Frolic in slumber beneath celestial beams,
Whispers of starlight, quite silly and tough,
Sending us off with the wildest of dreams.

While planets play chess, oh what a sight,
With aliens giggling at their own game,
Glittering lullabies drift off into night,
And sleep comes a-knocking, "Hey, join my fame!"

Miracles Shining Through Winter's Embrace

Snowflakes are hustling, each one a twirl,
They gather together, a feathery crew,
Chasing hot chocolate, oh what a whirl,
Carrots for noses? They'll take a few!

Penguins in bow ties tap dance on ice,
Giving it all with a wintery flair,
Snowmen debate about sugar or spice,
While kids boots stomp with a clownish air.

Icicles shimmer like jewels in the sun,
As squirrels in scarves dress to dazzle us all,
Winning at snowball fights, oh what fun,
Their squeaks of triumph echo and call.

Miracles giggle through frosty delight,
As cocoa melts hearts, wrapping warmth so divine,
In this season of wonder, just hold on tight,
'Cause laughter and joy are the best winter wine!

A Symphony of Lights Across the Darkness

Fireflies gather with glowsticks and zest,
They want to host concerts in gardens of cheer,
With beats that are funky, they're simply the best,
Making the night come alive, never fear.

The moon jives along, in a shimmery suit,
While stars shimmy-shake like they're in a dance,
A symphony ringing in each joyful toot,
Even crickets join in, giving tunes a chance.

Now rabbits in tuxedos sway to the sound,
As hedgehogs play trumpets, who knew they could?
With harmonies rising, oh what joy abound,
Critters unite as they dance in the wood.

A rhythm that sparkles in every tight spin,
As night wraps around us, oh what a sight,
In darkness, the music makes everyone grin,
Let's celebrate all with a symphony bright!

Wishes Manifested in Starlit Silence

In the quietest night, a wish takes its flight,
With sparkles and giggles, it zooms through the sky,
Landing on rooftops, oh what pure delight,
Jumping with joy as it whispers, "I'll try!"

A cat in pajamas dreams big while it naps,
Imagining castles for fuzzy little mice,
Each wish tailors magic; it springs from the gaps,
Like love notes scribbled on candy, not ice!

With each starlit breath, our dreams dance around,
They bounce like balloons, so cheerful and bright,
In silence, they giggle, with no sullen sound,
Whispers of wishes under the moonlight.

What if a unicorn made it all true?
With sprinkles and laughter, oh, what a scene!
They twirl through the night, just me and you,
In starlit silence, living out dreams supreme!

A Tapestry of Kindness and Cheer

Woven threads of humor bright,
A smile can take a silly flight.
Jokes that dance on air so light,
Bringing laughter, pure delight.

From kind friends who share their snack,
To pets who chase their own tail back.
Life's quirks make us laugh with glee,
Embracing joy, just wait and see.

Mismatched socks and silly hats,
Singing loudly with the cats.
Kindness wrapped in laughter's fold,
A tapestry of cheer, behold!

So raise a glass and toast the fun,
With friends like these, we've already won!
We weave our joy, we plant our cheer,
In this bright tapestry, year after year.

Illuminated by Kindred Spirits

With friends who share your goofy fate,
Life's a dance, can't be late.
Laughter echoes, spirits soar,
Together we can always explore.

In spirit realms, we find our grace,
Twinkling tales, a comic chase.
From "oops, I tripped" to silly spills,
Kindred hearts, we share our thrills.

Every giggle is a spark,
Lighting up the dull and dark.
In every heart there shines a jest,
In foolishness, we find our best.

So hold your friends, laugh loud and clear,
In moments shared, we have no fear.
Together we're a merry band,
Illuminated, hand in hand.

Starlit Pathways to Joy

Underneath the glowing stars,
We strut like we're in fancy cars.
Taking steps with silly flair,
Dancing dreams float through the air.

In starlit glow, we sing our songs,
With goofy moves that can't be wrong.
Each twinkle promises a cheer,
Joyful hearts are always near.

Falling over, giggles burst,
In life's grand play, we quench our thirst.
For laughter lights the darkest night,
On pathways paved in pure delight.

So grab a friend, and off we go,
With joy to share, our spirits glow.
In every laugh, we find our way,
Starlit joy, come what may.

The Glow of Memory and Wonder

A box of treasures made of dreams,
Filled with laughter and silly schemes.
Each memory a glowing light,
Shining bright, feels just so right.

From quirky trips and funny tales,
To bread that flops and wind that wails.
We find our glow in silly places,
With goofy grins on all our faces.

As time rolls on, we reminisce,
In every laugh, a little bliss.
The glow of memory, shining clear,
With friends beside, we have no fear.

So gather 'round, let stories flow,
In the warmth of friendship's glow.
For life's a ride, a wondrous spree,
In the glow of love, we are free.

The Glow of Compassion in the Chill

In a world so cold, a smile can thaw,
A warmth that spreads, like butter on raw.
When friends lend a hand, or shout with glee,
Compassion's glow, it warms you and me.

A cat prances by, wearing a hat,
Saying, 'What's cooler? Me or the rat?'
Laughter erupts, as snowflakes fall,
Compassion shines bright, it out-glows them all.

Hot cocoa shared, with marshmallows afloat,
Who knew that kindness could also promote?
In every sweet sip, a hug in disguise,
The glow of compassion, it never dies.

So when winter bites, and the world turns grey,
Spread kindness like glitter, let it play.
For in the chill, you'll find the warm,
Compassion's glow, it breaks every norm.

Whimsical Wonders Under the Night's Veil

The moon winks down, with a mischievous grin,
As owls hoot softly, let the fun begin!
Stars dance above, wearing sparkly shoes,
A night full of wonder, no time for the blues.

A raccoon in shades, with a flair for the bold,
Steals sandwiches gently, with stories untold.
Fireflies twinkle, like fairy lights bright,
Whimsical wonders fill the delight.

A skunk tells a joke, just to break the gloom,
While a hedgehog juggles, oh what a show!
Under the night's veil, adventure unfolds,
In this whimsical world, who needs gold?

So laugh with the night, let your spirit soar,
Adventure awaits, just step out the door!
Whimsical wonders, they linger and weave,
Under the moon, we always believe.

Starlit Pathways to Warm Memories

Walking on pathways lit by starlight,
Each step whispers tales of laughter and fright.
Memories twinkle like stars in the sky,
Making us giggle as time passes by.

Silly socks worn on a chilly day,
Dance in the moonbeams, come out to play.
A mishap with pie, a face full of cream,
Starlit pathways, where memories gleam.

With friends gathered 'round, telling old tales,
Of mischief and laughter that never fails.
The warmth of the past in bright constellation,
Starlit pathways spark sweet celebration.

So come fearlessly, just follow those lights,
Where laughter echoes through magical nights.
In starlit pathways, warmth is the prize,
A treasure of memories that always ties.

A Time for Togetherness Under Twinkling Skies

Under twinkling skies, a gathering cheer,
Friends all around, the meaning is clear.
Each face aglow, in the warm evening air,
A time for togetherness, nothing compares.

With pies on the table, and jokes shared aloud,
We laugh until tears make us feel so proud.
A dance with a squirrel, who knows all the moves,
Togetherness grooves, oh how it improves!

The stars play a tune that makes our hearts sway,
To the rhythm of friendship, we join in the play.
Hot drinks in hand, as we share all our tales,
Under twinkling skies, warmth never fails.

So here's to the nights when laughter's in bloom,
To friends and to joy, may they fill every room.
In this time of togetherness, let spirits rise,
Under twinkling skies, it's the best of goodbyes.

Illuminated Spirits Celebrating the Season

In the glow of neon lights,
We toast with mugs of cheer,
Sipping cocoa, feeling bright,
Ignoring all our holiday fear.

The Christmas tree's all decked out,
With ornaments that mostly fall,
Tinsel battles with the cat,
As we embrace the festive sprawl.

Uncle Joe's impromptu dance,
Causes quite the awkward scene,
While Grandma takes a second glance,
At the mistletoe so keen.

With carols sung off-key and loud,
We laugh till we can't breathe,
In this zany, jolly crowd,
We find the joys we weave.

Chasing Shadows of Light Through the Winter

Snowflakes dance, we run amok,
In boots too big, we trip and fall,
Creating snowmen that look like ducks,
And chasing shadows on the wall.

The sun sets early, skies are gray,
Yet our spirits shine so bright,
Forging hot cocoa heart-shaped trays,
With marshmallows that take flight.

We're bundled up, looking like bears,
With scarves that tie us in a knot,
Our laughter echoes through the airs,
While we forget to winter trot.

As winter whispers nippy tales,
We dance in boots, oh what a sight,
In this season, laughter prevails,
Chasing shadows with delight.

A Glimmer of Hope on Dark Nights

In the midst of winter's chill,
We light a candle, bright and gay,
Its flicker gives our hearts a thrill,
As we chase the gloom away.

With snowflakes falling soft and light,
We gather 'round with cheerful grins,
Sharing stories late at night,
Where each tale brings warmth within.

A glass of cheer, a raise of toast,
To moments we will treasure long,
For in this darkness, we can boast,
That laughter is our winter song.

So let the cold winds howl and shout,
We'll dance until the morning bright,
With cozy hearts, we'll scream and shout,
A glimmer shines through the dark night.

Glistening Heartbeats in The Frost

In the early morn, the world is still,
The frost glistens like a diamond,
We bundle up, with laughter's thrill,
As winter's wonderland descends.

With rosy cheeks and noses bright,
We race on sleds, a wild spree,
Tumbling down with pure delight,
As snowflakes dance and set us free.

Hot soup and hugs, the perfect blend,
With every sip, we feel the glow,
In cozy nooks, we make amends,
And let those frosty worries go.

So here's to joy in every frost,
Where heartbeats warm the chilly air,
In laughter, we find what was lost,
Glistening bright, beyond compare.

A Wonderland of Gleaming Stars

In a garden where stars wear hats,
And squirrels dance with silly spats,
The moon sways like a jellyfish,
While comets cook a tasty dish.

The owls spin tales with flapping wings,
As rabbits play the tambourine and sing,
Each star a spark of playful cheer,
In this wonderland, no one sheds a tear.

Bouncing beams of light do prance,
While fluffy clouds host a teddy bear dance,
The horizon giggles and gives a shout,
In a gleaming starland, there's never a doubt.

Here, laughter bounces like a ball,
With giggles echoing through the hall,
So grab your towel for a cosmic dip,
In the sparkling pool of a starry trip.

Whimsical Dreams in Celestial Colors

In candyfloss clouds with rainbow beams,
Fish ride bicycles, or so it seems,
Fluffy unicorns wear polka dot clothes,
Sharing secrets that only the jellybeans knows.

The stars play hopscotch across the skies,
And giggling planets are in disguise,
Each comet's tail is a colorful show,
As they dance through the galaxy, to and fro.

Silly sea otters sing to the moon,
While astronauts play a goofy tune,
Twinkling lights in a parade do glide,
In whimsical dreams where laughter won't hide.

With bubbles of joy floating in the night,
The world spins in pure delight,
So come along to this cosmic night,
Where dreams are bright and spirits take flight.

A Symphony of Joyful Lights

The stars play music with silver strings,
While dandelions wear tiny crowns and sing,
Fireflies dance with tiny tap shoes,
In a harmony of light, no one can lose.

Galaxies twirl in a grand ballet,
As the sun hums a cheerful ray,
The moon holds a concert with string beans,
In a symphony of colors, where laughter leans.

Planets stomp in rhythm quite loud,
As asteroids leap, joining the crowd,
Neon lights flash in a gleeful spree,
Making melodies that set us free.

So grab your pals for a night full of cheer,
As joyful lights twinkle brightly near,
In the universe's orchestra, we belong,
Playing together, dancing along.

Gathering Under Cosmic Glimmer

Underneath the stars, we gather round,
With cookies and cakes piled high on the ground,
The planets chuckle and join our feast,\nIn this cosmic
gathering, joy is released.

Martians bring jello in shades of green,
While space cows jump, a sight to be seen,
Aliens play hopscotch with shooting stars,
As we dance beneath the twinkly guitars.

The Milky Way shimmers, a blanket of light,
As we roast marshmallows, oh what a sight,
Our laughter echoes among the bright beams,
In a galaxy filled with whimsical dreams.

So take a seat by the cosmic fire,
Where joy and wonder never tire,
Under a canopy of light, we align,
In this cosmic glimmer, all hearts entwine.

The Glow of Warmth Amidst the Chill

The fire crackles, pop and snap,
I burn the toast, oh what a trap!
Socks mismatched, a fashion crime,
I'm just glad it's not dinner time.

Hot cocoa spilling, marshmallows float,
My dog steals the cookies, what a goat!
Blankets piled up, a cozy fort,
To be a kid again, my favorite sport.

Fingers frozen, but heart's ablaze,
With jokes and laughter through the haze.
Oh, winter nights are pure delight,
Especially when I forget the light!

So here's to warmth in fireside cheer,
With friends so close, there's naught to fear.
Though jack frost nips, I take a stand,
Laughing at winter, hot drink in hand.

Festive Euphoria in the Midnight Blue

The stars are twinkling, oh what a sight,
Pine trees decked out, looking so bright.
Tinsel fiddles, and ornaments sway,
I lost my pants while dancing, they say!

Carols ringing, but what's that tune?
Singing off-key like a wild raccoon.
Cookies baking, flour on my nose,
I blame my cat, who also knows.

Lights on the roof, oh what a mess,
I tripped and fell, oh what duress!
But laughter echoes through the night,
As we all try to get the lights right.

In this midnight blue, all souls unite,
With joy and cheer, we take to flight.
For in the festive, all can be found,
Even the joyous, silly and crowned!

Joyful Echoes in the December Breeze

Snowflakes fumble in a windy waltz,
I try to catch one, but who faults?
Laughter rings out, a cheerful sound,
While icy puddles trap me on the ground.

Children bundled up, like sausage rolls,
Making snowmen, with goofy goals.
Their carrot noses, a shaky fit,
And snowballs flying, well, that's legit!

Brace yourselves, the chill does bite,
But cocoa warms us, oh what a sight!
While outside it's freezing, inside it glows,
With visions of cookies, marshmallow flows.

So let's embrace this winter cheer,
With playful mirth, and joy sincere.
For laughter lingers like a sweet breeze,
In December's heart, we find our ease.

Illuminated Hearts Under Snowy Veils

Under snowy veils, we stroll in a daze,
Losing our hats in the frosty glaze.
Outfit mismatched, a snowsuit trend,
But laughter brings warmth, oh joyous blend.

Old ornaments hang, some hang by a thread,
Grandma's recipes make us well-fed.
But one bite too many lands me on the floor,
My stomach protesting, but I want more!

Twinkling lights flicker, they dance like our feet,
As we waltz through winter, cold and sweet.
Who says we can't be a little absurd?
Joyful echoes, every laugh preferred.

So let's raise a cup, to snowflakes and cheer,
To all heartfelt glimmers, and memories dear.
In this frosty affair, may our souls bind,
Illuminated hearts, warmth intertwined.

Bright Horizons on Frosty Evenings

The snowflakes dance, a clumsy crew,
They tumble down, in black and blue.
With hats too big and scarves too long,
They laugh and slip, it's a slapstick song.

The kettle's whistling, it's time for tea,
A fluffy cat jumps, thinks it's a flea.
With cozy socks and grinning smiles,
We toast to warmth, for a few more miles.

The icicles drip, like a frozen beard,
A snowman waves, but no one's cheered.
His carrot nose is kind of rogue,
As birds fly by, giving him a joke.

So here we sit on frosty nights,
In mismatched jammies, with cheesy delights.
Bright horizons wait, though it's cold outside,
We'll sip and giggle, with snow our guide.

Miracles Wrapped in Stardust

A shooting star crossed the sky so fast,
The cat just blinked; she thought it a cast!
Miracles happen on lazy nights,
When socks are lost and nothing feels right.

Wrapped in stardust, the pizza awaits,
So we grab a slice and all contemplate.
Life's little magic, like cheese in a pull,
Stretched out tales where time is a lull.

With giggles and dreams swirling all around,
Like popcorn popping without making a sound.
We toast to the mess of the cosmic feast,
With each joyful hiccup, we're kind of a beast!

In pajamas we sit, a spectacular sight,
Dancing to music no one else might.
Miracles wrapped, in laughter and cheer,
In this stardust party, we hold life so dear.

The Light of Togetherness

When the lights dim down, and laughter begins,
We gather 'round, it's where the fun spins.
A game of charades, with faces so bright,
It's hard to gauge what's wrong or what's right.

The dog joins in, thinking it's a fair,
As grandma's tea spills, but no one would care.
With pies like mountains and laughter so loud,
We create our warmth, a whimsical crowd.

Our bright little quirks, put together like mash,
With tickles and pokes, it's quite the splash!
In the light of togetherness, we find our glow,
With silly mishaps making the show.

So let's raise our cups to the moments we share,
To laughter, to warmth, and love in the air.
For in this bright chaos, our hearts intertwine,
We shine even brighter when we're a bit blind.

Festive Reflections in the Night Sky

Twinkling lights dangle, all merry and bright,
The cat goes berserk, thinking it's night flight.
With ornaments on branches, an adventure begins,
As popcorn strings sway, creating small sins.

Beneath the mistletoe, a sly grin appears,
Two left feet dance through the joy and the cheers.
With cookies and milk, an odd mix of treats,
We're baking disaster, and everyone eats!

The snowman's arms wave, they're rather unsteady,
As relatives argue about who's more ready.
In festive reflections, we gather so close,
To fill up the globe with laughter, like most.

So here's to the chaos, the love that we feel,
With warmth in our hearts, and a wintery meal.
The night sky above, full of glitters and whys,
In our little corner, pure joy never dies.

The Warmth of Love Beneath the Cold

When winter winds begin to blow,
We snuggle close, our faces aglow.
With hot cocoa and cheesy jokes,
Even snowmen laugh at our pokes.

There's warmth in love, it's oh so nice,
Like finding a forgotten slice.
In frozen times, we make a scene,
Two frozen fools in a love machine.

The frosty air brings chilly cheer,
While we sip tea, we'll conquer fear.
The world outside may freeze and crack,
But here inside, there's no lack!

So let the snowflakes dance around,
We'll make a fortress, safe and sound.
With every hug, the cold can't bite,
Our hearts keep warm, through winter's night.

Light and Laughter in the Evening Dew

The evening dew plays hide and seek,
With giggles soft, it's all we speak.
As crickets play their fading song,
We twirl around, where we belong.

The fireflies join in on the fun,
They blink and dance, on the run.
Our laughter echoes through the night,
A symphony of pure delight.

We spot the moon, he winks at me,
"Keep it light, be wild and free!"
With every sip of fizzy drink,
We toast to stars and dreams we think.

With laughter ringing, hearts will flow,
In the evening dew, love will grow.
Let's skip and jump, run wild and free,
In this tiny world, just you and me.

A Magical Soirée Amidst the Stars

Beneath the stars, we set the scene,
With snacks and drinks, it's fit for a queen.
We twirl in dresses made of light,
A soirée that lasts through the night.

The cupcakes sparkle, with stars on top,
While laughter erupts and we can't stop.
We dance with shadows in moonlit beams,
Living the moments of our wildest dreams.

A squirrel is our DJ, he's quite the pro,
With every spin, our joy will grow.
The constellations lend us their glow,
While we drink punch from an old garden hoe.

As midnight strikes, we make a wish,
In this magical moment, let's not hiss.
With sparkling eyes and carefree hearts,
This soirée will bring us endless starts.

Embracing the Spirit of Giving and Light

With open arms, we gather near,
Wrapped in love, we spread good cheer.
We light the lamps and spark the glow,
Sharing smiles, it's the best show.

From cookies baked to toys that shine,
We give from hearts that ever align.
A sprinkle of joy on each delight,
Turning grumpy frowns to pure delight.

As laughter echoes through the halls,
We sing our tunes, let joy enthrall.
Giving's magic makes our hearts grow,
In every hug, the love will flow.

So let's embrace this spirit bright,
With little deeds that shine so light.
For in this world, we find the key,
A little love, sets our hearts free.

Starlight Serenades on Winter's Breath

The snowflakes dance with cheeky grins,
Waiting for winter to roll on in.
Hot cocoa spills, oh what a mess,
As I slip on ice, I must confess!

The stars above are winking bright,
While I'm wrapped up, what a sight!
Singing carols with a snowman friend,
His frozen smile will never end!

Each breath puffs out like little clouds,
Squirrelly dreams where are my crowds?
In this frosty, giggly embrace,
Winter's charm is a silly race!

So here's to nights so pure and clear,
With laughter spilling, full of cheer.
Let's toast to stars, the cold, and glee,
And hope tomorrow brings more spree!

Echoes of Delight in Shimmering Skies

Look up high, the clouds have fun,
They're pillow-fighting when day is done.
A giggle here, a twinkle there,
In this cozy, magical air!

Jellybean dreams drift on by,
In sugar-coated spaces, oh my!
Riding rainbows on a mock orange,
My heart's ablaze, what a torch!

The moon is winking, playing tricks,
While I'm just looking for some kicks.
Stars are falling, what a blight,
Did I just catch one? What a sight!

So let's rejoice, shout out our cheer,
For winter's glow, we hold dear.
With echoes of laughter, we'll sing our song,
In shimmering skies where we all belong!

Mirthful Reflections on a Snowy Summary

Snowmen wear hats with silly styles,
Making me laugh for a hundred miles.
They wobble and giggle as they sway,
I think they might just steal the day!

In snowball fights, I lose my might,
And stumble over, what a sight!
With rosy cheeks and running nose,
Winter pranks are how it goes!

The trees are dressed in frosting white,
While birds are chirping, pure delight.
Sledding down hills, I fly up high,
Winter's essence never says goodbye!

So wrap me tight in blankets warm,
As outside the snowflakes swirl and swarm.
I'll hum a tune, snicker with glee,
Mirthful reflections, just you and me!

Candles and Constellations: A Whimsical Bond

Candles flicker with tales untold,
Whispering secrets that never grow old.
With every glow, dreams start to bloom,
As I trip over a rogue vacuum!

Constellations twirl in the night,
Twirking stars, what a silly sight!
They guide my way with a giggle and cheer,
While I search for munchies, oh dear!

The aroma of cookies fills the air,
Baking mishaps cause me to stare!
With frosting mustaches, we all partake,
In this snowy bond, we make no mistake!

So light a candle, and sing with me,
As we dance among the bright and free.
With laughter echoing all around,
In this whimsical bond, joy knows no bound!

The Spirit of the Season in Soft Radiance

In the rush of the holiday cheer,
Spruce trees sparkle, cold and clear.
Cookies baked in grandma's pot,
Burned on the edge, but they still hit the spot.

Jingle bells ringing, kids run amok,
One trip on a sleigh, oh what a shock!
Hot cocoa spills on the festive rug,
Mom's not amused, but the kids just shrug.

Socks on the line, like colorful whales,
Unicorns tangled in tinsel trails.
Light fights in the living room, oh what a sight,
Grandpa's nap time turns into a fright.

Yet in the chaos, warmth we find,
Laughter and love, forever intertwined.
In this soft glow, we dance and sing,
Tales of the season, our hearts they bring.

Echoes of Laughter in the Crisp Air

Snowflakes falling like popcorn from sky,
Kids building snowmen, one foot and one eye.
They smile and they giggle, frosty delight,
Till the snowman collapses—oh, what a sight!

Roasted chestnuts, the street vendor's call,
While auntie slips on ice and begins to sprawl.
The laughter erupts, it echoes so loud,
As we gather together, a merry crowd.

Hot soup in hand, while scarves never stay,
The dog steals a roll and runs far away.
With each muffled giggle and soft chilly breeze,
In crisp air we flourish, nothing's quite as easy.

As daylight retreats and darkness takes hold,
Stories unfold, both funny and old.
In the hearts of the season, joy is our share,
Echoes of laughter fill up the cold air.

Embracing the Glow of Generosity

Gift lists are long, with cheap plastic toys,
A parade of colors, a choir of joys.
Uncle Joe wrapped a brick for Auntie Claire,
Now we all question just how much he cares.

Dinners abound with mountains of food,
But Aunt Peg's mystery casserole's mood.
With each heavenly bite, we fake smiles of bliss,
While dreaming of nuggets, we secretly miss.

And yet in the chaos, hearts grow so wide,
Sharing what's precious, standing side by side.
In all of our blunders, the warmth we ignite,
Generosity glows in the soft winter night.

So raise up your glasses, let's toast to the fun,
Among all our follies, our spirits have run.
In this season of giving, let's take a chance,
With laughter and love, let's join in the dance.

Twinkling Dreams Spun in Celestial Threads

Stars sprinkle down like confetti from space,
We try to catch one, but we fall on our face.
Whispers of wishes float high above,
While cats pounce on lights like they're in love.

Dreams spun in colors, every hue bright,
As socks disappear in the wash every night.
With each frenzied search, we bicker and blame,
The cat's the real culprit, we'll never be the same.

Elf hats on heads, wobbly and tall,
We pose for a picture, and one takes a fall.
Laughter erupts with twinkling delight,
Creating moments that feel just right.

In this season of dreams, we twirl and we sway,
Each misfit moment makes bright our gray day.
So dance under stars, let your heart fully tread,
In the glow of our laughter, all worries we shred.

Radiance of Yuletide Dreams

The snowman stands with a goofy grin,
Wearing my hat, now he thinks he's in!
Sipping cocoa, he spills with glee,
Wondering why he doesn't melt for me.

The tree's all aglow with ornaments bright,
Except for that one that just took flight.
A cat named Whiskers takes her leap,
And the whole thing crashes with a squeak!

Cookies left out for Santa's delight,
But my sister sneaks one in plain sight.
"Merry Christmas!" she chews without care,
While I just stare, my mouth in a glare.

Rudolph's nose shines with a wink and a blink,
As he guzzles milk, oh, what do you think?
He's on a diet but loves dessert,
Now he's got a belly quite hard to avert!

Celestial Glitter Above the Hearth

The stars above twinkle, oh so bold,
Whispering secrets that never get old.
But look closely, there's a comet's trail,
And it's wearing socks—what a curious tale!

The fireplace crackles with laughter and cheer,
As grandpa tells jokes that we've all heard here.
His punchline is stale, but we all still laugh,
While the dog rolls over, our little better half!

A stocking hangs low, filled with sweet snacks,
Except for the pickle! Who thought of that?
We'll find it on New Year's, that's for sure,
Sitting on a shelf, our holiday tour!

Mistletoe sways in the drafty hall,
A means for smooches, or maybe not at all.
Cousin Bob tries to steal a quick kiss,
But ends up with auntie instead, what a twist!

Laughter Wrapped in Silver Twilight

Under the twinkling silver lights,
We sip hot cocoa, sharing delights.
But who is that sneaking a marshmallow?
It's Uncle Jerry, dressed like a fellow!

The snowflakes dance in the edge of night,
While grandpa spins tales that are out of sight.
Angels on rooftops think it's a show,
As they cheer him on with a jolly ho-ho!

The sleigh is parked, full of silly sights,
With rubber chickens and sparkling lights.
Oh, but don't tell Santa what's inside,
He's still recovering from last year's ride!

With giggles and joy, we all gather round,
As laughter erupts with each quirky sound.
The holiday spirit dances with zest,
In a world where silliness is the best!

Starlit Wishes on a Silent Night

The moon's so bright it shimmers and glows,
Lighting up reindeer with glittery bows.
We try to be quiet, just tiptoe a bit,
But the cat jumps high and lands right on his wit!

Presents are wrapped with tape everywhere,
Oh, how we wish for a magic repair.
With bows on the floor and paper galore,
It looks like a tornado dashed through the floor!

The fireplace pops like popcorn in flight,
While I wrestle a ribbon that's caught me tight.
Little bro giggles, he thinks it's a game,
As I wind up wrapped, with a newfound fame!

Wishing on stars, we hope they come true,
For a life filled with laughter and more silly too.
In this Yuletide glow, we dance with delight,
As memories shimmer through this beautiful night!

Celestial Kindness in the Winter Breeze

In winter's chill, I found a sight,
A snowman with a carrot nose so bright.
He waved his stick arm, oh what a tease,
'Thank you, kind human, for this winter breeze.'

The squirrels don coats; they fashion their hats,
They giggle and chatter, sharing some chats.
A little snowflake lands on my cheek,
It melts with a wink, oh winter, you sneak!

Hot cocoa's brewing, marshmallows in flight,
A snow angel flops—what a frosty delight.
The stars look down with a twinkle and grin,
They love this season; let the fun begin!

So here's to kindness in icy domains,
Where laughter and warmth break all winter's chains.
We'll dance in the snow, let our spirits soar,
Winter's a playground, who could ask for more?

Radiance of Unity Amidst Frosty Moments

The family gathered, the fire aglow,
With each silly story, the laughter will flow.
Grandma's retelling of snowball fights,
And Uncle Bob's snowman with googly sights.

The dog wore a sweater, too tight, oh dear!
He pranced around like he just had a beer.
With snowflakes as confetti for our holiday cheer,
We embrace winter's frosty chandeliers.

Hot cider is served in mismatched old cups,
As we slip and we slide, trying not to trip up.
Together we smile, with snow in our hair,
Creating new memories, no moment to spare.

So let's toast to winter, to laughter and fun,
With unity shining, we're all number one.
In frosty moments, together we'll stand,
Radiance of joy—hand in joyful hand.

Echoing Laughter in a Winter Paradise

In a winter paradise, quiet and bright,
The kids roll in snowballs, an epic snow fight.
A snow fort appears, weapons all ready,
They declare it a battle, and all remain steady.

The icicles hang like daggers of glass,
The laughter erupts as the snowballs amass.
A dodge and a weave, oh what fun we create,
The winter reprieve is truly first-rate.

Then out comes the sleds with a whoosh and a glide,
We conquer the hill with a laugh and a slide.
Snowflakes like feathers dance through the air,
In this winter paradise, nothing compares.

As the sun sets low and the sky's painted gold,
We gather 'round fires as the stories unfold.
With echoing laughter to warm up the night,
Our winter delight feels oh-so-right!

A Journey Through Starlit Bliss

In the crisp winter night, under stars all aglow,
We stepped through the snow, our breath like a show.
The moon gently winked as we wandered the path,
Sharing secrets of joy, escaping the math.

Sipping on cocoa, our mittens were snug,
We spotted a reindeer, or was it a drug?
It pranced by us, pulling jingle-bell sleighs,
Oh, what a journey through magical ways!

With laughter that echoed like bells through the trees,
We danced in the moonlight, an exhilarating breeze.
Chasing the shadows, our spirits took flight,
In this starlit bliss, everything felt right.

So here's to the journey, the fun we embrace,
The simple delights that lighten our pace.
With snowflakes a-twirl and starlight's soft kiss,
We cherish these moments—in winter, pure bliss.

Milton Keynes UK
Ingram Content Group UK Ltd.
UKHW022311041224
452010UK00018B/780

9 789916 909850